# There Was An Old Woman...

## A Family Musical

## David Wood

A SAMUEL FRENCH ACTING EDITION

# SAMUEL FRENCH

FOUNDED 1830

SAMUELFRENCH-LONDON.CO.UK
SAMUELFRENCH.COM

ISBN 978-0-573-05051-0

www.samuelfrench-london.co.uk

www.samuelfrench.com

# THERE WAS AN OLD WOMAN....

First produced at the Haymarket Theatre, Leicester, by the Haymarket Theatre Company on Wednesday July 25th, 1979, with the following cast of characters:

| | |
|---|---|
| Cocky | David Learner |
| Mother Shipton | Carolyn Moody |
| Jill | Melanie Parr |
| Jack | Christopher Wenner |
| The Great Boon | Roy Macready |
| Giant | Christopher Scott |

The Children:

| Troupe A | Troupe B |
|---|---|
| Andrew Adeyemi | Adam Bentley |
| Andrew Alcock | Clive De'Ath |
| Christopher Alcock | Christopher Dewing |
| James Bedford | Grant Evatt |
| David Bloomfield | Shaun Fernandes |
| Matthew Brown | Andrew Hirst |
| Max Fraser | Robert Irwin |
| Robert Graves | Andrew King |
| Adrian Hockridge | Christopher Moulds |
| John Hockridge | Neil Muckle |
| Atul Patel | Stephen Nutter |
| Darren Smith | Paul Townsend |
| Earl Thomas | Christopher Whitfield |
| Robin Ward | Julie Allen |
| Sophia Alcock | Lisa Barnett |
| Sara Allen | Michelle Barrington |
| Sarah Blackwell | Michelle Butler |
| Tina Carr | Donna Deacon |
| Lindsey Charlton | Paula Deacon |
| Julia Donoghue | Ellen-Claire Dovey |
| Jocelyn Gerald | Rachael Drew |
| Kirti Gohil | Rachel Greasley |
| Nicole Louis | Lynne Page |
| Lisa Myatt | Karen Roper |
| Sara Riley | Vivien Sharman |
| Amanda Seekings | Angela Sharpe |
| Karen Smalley | Sonia Swaby |
| Lorraine Smyth | Liane Tidd |
| Johanne Thorpe | Caroline Underwood |
| Rebecca Valentine | Tracy Warren |
| Michelle Williams | Louise White |
| Claire Woolridge | Georgia Wilkes |

The play directed by Hugh Wooldridge
Designed by Clive Lavagna
Musical Direction by Ian Smith
Musical arrangements by David Carter

# MUSICAL NUMBERS

### ACT I

| | |
|---|---|
| 1. *Cockadoodle Doo/There Was An Old Woman* | Mother Shipton, Jack, Jill, Children, (Cocky) |
| 2. *The Giant in the Castle* | Mother Shipton, Jack, Jill, Children, (Cocky) |
| 3. *Two Spells a Day* | The Great Boon, Mother Shipton, Jack, Jill, Children, (Cocky) |
| 4. *Where's My Shoe?* | Giant |
| 4A. *Cockadoodle Doo/There Was An Old Woman* (reprise) | All |
| 5. *Grow* | The Great Boon, Mother Shipton, Jack, Jill, Children, (Cocky) |
| 6. *Till Today Becomes Tomorrow* | Mother Shipton or Jill, Jack, Children, Children, The Great Boon, (Cocky) |
| 6A. *Where's My Shoe?* (reprise) | Giant |
| 6B. *Cockadoodle Doo/There Was An Old Woman* (reprise) | All |

### ACT II

| | |
|---|---|
| 7. *Hushabye Giant* | Mother Shipton, Jack, Jill, The Great Boon, Children, (Cocky) |
| 8. *Creepy Crawly Cockypillar* | Children, Jack, Jill |
| 9. *The Show's The Thing (Part 1)* | Mother Shipton, The Great Boon, Jack, Jill, Children, (Cocky) |
| 10. *Finale* | All |
| 10A *Curtain Call—The Show's The Thing (Part 2)* | All |

*The song* The Show's The Thing *is included by kind permission of Tro-Essex Music, Ltd.*

*The Vocal Score for this family musical is on sale from Samuel French Ltd.*

## AUTHOR'S NOTES

Robin Midgley, of the Haymarket Theatre, Leicester, invited me to write *There Was An Old Woman* ... to fulfil a particular need. He wanted a play in which half-a-dozen actors would be joined by a team of local schoolchildren. The play would be musical, aimed at a family audience. The schoolchildren were to be used in an active capacity rather than as a choir, and their individual talents were to be allowed room to display themselves where possible. Robin suggested the rhyme, "There was an old woman who lived in a shoe ..." as a starting point. I agreed, and decided to have no qualms about plagiarizing relevant material from my earlier play *Old Mother Hubbard*, in which I had already introduced the idea of a mother and her children living in a shoe.

I hope the play will be found useful by professional repertory companies, involving the local community, as well as by amateur and school groups. Directors should note that the Circus in Act II is very important in terms of using the children's abilities—every production will naturally employ different ideas. In addition, throughout the play the children's group reactions will need special attention and control. I have purposely left them to a minimum in the text so that they can develop naturally from the situation.

D.W.

## SET

The basic set involves a large shoe or boot in which Mother Shipton and all the Children live. It has therefore been adapted to look like a house or cottage, with windows, a door, a chimney, plants etc. The shoe is in a clearing, possibly with trees surrounding. As the shoe has to "disappear", it should be mobile, and it is suggested that a cyclorama forms a backcloth, which can be flown out to accommodate the shoe's exit; or the shoe can go into the wings. One brief scene is played with a traditional-style well on a hill, under a none-too-healthy apple tree. This could all be on one small truck; it never appears when the shoe is on.

## CHARACTERS

| | |
|---|---|
| **Mother Shipton** | warm, lovable, eccentric, excitable traditional figure—(could be played by a man if required) |
| **Jack** | idle, lovable, a bit slow-witted |
| **Jill** | her common sense compensates for Jack's ineffectual nature—she takes the lead much more than him; almost tomboyish |
| **The Great Boon** | travelling magician, dressed in what one would expect a magician to look like, complete with cloak. Extrovert *entrepreneur*. His enthusiasm makes up for his occasional lack of *real* magical skill (but his *tricks* should be good) |
| **Cocky** | the family pet cockerel; cannot speak, only "crow" or "cock-a-doodle-doo" to wake everyone up. Should be appealing and funny with a distinctive strut and bird-like movement. Could be played by a male or female |
| **Giant** | we only *see* the Giant when he has been reduced to human size by the Great Boon's magic. But when he is his normal gigantic size, we hear his deep booming voice (over speakers) and occasionally see giant prop feet. In his reduced shape he looks like a traditional giant, shaggy hair and beard, carrying a club etc., taller than average to make him menacing even when so comparatively small |

| | |
|---|---|
| **Mini-Giant** | a miniature version of the Giant, *played by a small child*, but dressed identically—complete with beard |
| **The Children** | there can be as many children as practicable. Their *real* names should be used; perhaps the names could be written on their T-shirts. |

# NOTES ON THE GREAT BOON'S MAGIC

*It may be of help to invite the assistance of a local magician to teach and advise the actor playing The Great Boon. However, the following are suggestions of methods to achieve the effects required.*

1   *THE GREAT BOON'S FLOWER PRODUCTIONS are probably best done with "feather bouquets" from a magic shop. These can be sleeved.*

2   *RESTORED SHOELACE: probably the easiest method is to use rope magnets or "poppers", which simply join the two ends, making the rope look whole. The Great Boon "joins" the ends under cover of his hand.*

3   *GHOST TO WITCH ILLUSION. First, the act as the audience sees and hears it:*

**The Great Boon** And now, may I kindly beg, borrow or steal two young members of the audience? (*He selects a boy and girl from the children*) You and you? Thank you. What are your names? Ann and Guy. Together we are going to tell the incredible tale of the Witch and the Ghost. Ann, will you play the Witch? Please enter my caravan and put on your costume. (*To Mother Shipton*) Perhaps you madam, would help her.

**Mother Shipton** Certainly, Mr Great Boon.

*Mother Shipton stands by the entrance to the caravan, apparently supervising all the changes.*

**The Great Boon** And Guy, would you like to play the Ghost? Have you ever been a Ghost before? Show me how you might haunt somebody. (*He carries on ad lib. if necessary until Ann is ready*)

*The "Witch" comes out of the caravan*

Ah, splendid, here is the Witch. Ann, are you all right in there?

*The "Witch" nods*

Off you go, Guy.

*Guy enters the caravan*

Now, this story concerns a wicked Witch who lived alone in a cottage in the forest. She practised her magic spells all day, and all night flew through the sky on her broomstick. Hey, you haven't a broomstick ...

*The "Ghost" comes out of the caravan*

Ah, here's Guy the Ghost. All right in there, Guy?

*The "Ghost" nods*

Ann, back you go and find your broomstick.

*The "Witch" returns to the caravan*

Now, Guy, you are a ghost who is very, very hungry, and one day knocks on the door of the Wicked Witch's cottage.

*The "Witch" returns from the caravan with a broomstick. From now on, the two Children act out The Great Boon's words*

Knock, knock, knock. The Witch answered. "Please," said the Ghost, "I'm so hungry, can you spare some food? Anything." "Well," said the Wicked Witch, "do you like cold mutton stew?" "M'm, yes," said the Ghost. "Then come back tomorrow," cackled the Witch. "It's hot now!" And she slammed the door in the Ghost's face. The Ghost was furious, and thought hard of a way to get his own back. He was so hungry. If he could only get inside the cottage, he could eat. Well, the *Witch* was inside the cottage, so all he had to do was to change places with her. By magic. So he concentrated hard and uttered the magic words—

*Drum roll*

Piggledy Higgledy
Fidgetty Itch
May I change places
With the Witch!

*The Great Boon "fluences" the "Ghost" and the "Witch". Dramatic build-up. First, the "Witch" is revealed to be Guy; second, the "Ghost" is revealed to be Ann. Fanfare chords proclaim the trick has worked. The two Children return to the caravan to take off their "Ghost" and "Witch" clothes.*

*The secret lies in the fact that there are in fact three children used, and three costumes—two "Witch" costumes and one "Ghost" costume. These costumes all have full hoods to cover the heads, with just two holes for the eyes. They are loose-fitting, to allow for easy putting-on over the children's other costumes. One girl, say "Jean", dressed in a "Witch" costume, is hidden in the caravan from the start. When Ann enters the caravan, Jean in fact emerges, and everyone assumes she must be Ann. Meanwhile, Ann prepares to put on the "Ghost" costume. When Guy enters the caravan, it is Ann who emerges as the "Ghost", not he. Guy puts on the second "Witch" costume, and when Jean returns into the caravan to find the broomstick, it is in fact Guy who emerges as the "Witch", carrying the broomstick. So now the change of places has been achieved: Ann is the "Ghost" and Guy is the "Witch"—and after the spell the magical transformation can be revealed. N.B. All three children should be the same height. They should take care not to make noises in the caravan or rock it when changing—especially at times when no-one is meant to be inside! Mother Shipton can be of help supervising the changes.*

4 *THE DISAPPEARANCE OF THE MINI-GIANT. A magical adviser could probably suggest more exotic ways of doing this illusion—disappearing from a sword cabinet, for example—but one simple way is to "vanish" him from a cabinet. This could be The Great Boon's caravan, which could lift off its wheels for the purpose. The inside should be painted black, and at*

*the back is a false panel or curtain, giving him a narrow hiding-place behind. The Mini-Giant is placed inside and the door or curtain closed. Seconds later the door is opened and he has disappeared. Instantaneously, a "double" Mini-Giant appears wherever required, e.g., at the back of the auditorium. This double Mini-Giant should be easy to provide, with the beard and shaggy hair. Another method is to put the Mini-Giant into a cabinet on a small podium. He hides in the podium as the cabinet is hoisted up in the air. The podium (and Mini-Giant) is pushed off stage. Then the cabinet is shown to be empty by falling apart. Showmanship is of the essence here. If a really unusual or complicated illusion is required, a magical adviser is the best answer.*

# ACT I

*The* CURTAIN *rises on, or the audience see as they enter the auditorium, a very large shoe or boot. It takes up a major part of the stage, and appears to be in a sort of clearing or forest glade, surrounded by trees, some of which are jagged, as if trampled over by a giant. The shoe has been adapted to look like a house or cottage, with windows, a door, a chimney, plants in window boxes or hanging baskets, etc. The shoe should, however, be mobile, because it has to "disappear"; perhaps a cyclorama forms a backcloth, which can be flown out to accommodate the shoe's exit, or the shoe could go into the wings*

It is dawn. *Music, as the lights creep up casting interesting shapes and shadows on the shoe*

*Cocky enters, making clucking noises as he ruffles his feathers and wakes up. The audience should find his strutting and occasional pecking at the ground amusing. He takes up a crowing position near the door, and prepares himself by clearing his throat*

**Cocky** Cockadoodle doo! Cockadoodle doooooo! (*He looks at the door for a reaction. Nothing. He starts again*)

Cockadood ... (*He is interrupted by the door opening*)

*Mother Shipton enters yawning and perhaps putting on her shawl*

**Mother Shipton** All right, Cocky! I heard you the first time. And the second.

*Cocky pecks her with kisses*

Good morning to you, too.

*More pecks*

Ooh, what a friendly fowl you are.

*More pecks*

All right, all right. Don't get carried away. Wake the children, please.

*Cocky poses in front of the door again*

**Cocky** Cockadoodle doo!


SONG 1: **Cockadoodle Doo/There was an Old Woman**

*The names of the children should be the cast's real names—except for Jack and Jill*

| **Mother Shipton** | Cockadoodle Doo |
| *Singing* | It's time to get up, there are jobs to do |
| | I'm gonna sweep the sole |
| | Cockadoodle Doo. |
| *(Calling)* | Jill, Ian, William, Sarah, George |

*Group 1 emerges sleepily from the shoe. All greet Mother Shipton*

| **Group 1** | Cockadoodle Doo |
| | It's time to get up, there are jobs to do |
| | We're gonna polish the toe |
| **Mother Shipton** | I'm gonna sweep the sole |
| **All** | Cockadoodle Doo. |
| **Mother Shipton** | Jane, Philip, Helen, Guy, Lucy |
| *(calling)* | |

*Group 2 enters*

| **Group 2** | Cockadoodle Doo |
| | It's time to get up, there are jobs to do |
| | We're gonna scrub the heel |
| **Group 1** | We're gonna polish the toe |
| **Mother Shipton** | I'm gonna sweep the sole |
| **All** | Cockadoodle Doo. |
| **Mother Shipton** | Jackie, John, Jean, David, Ann |
| *(calling)* | |

*Group 3 enters*

| **Group 3** | Cockadoodle Doo |
| | It's time to get up, there are jobs to do |
| | We're gonna shake the sheets |
| **Group 2** | We're gonna scrub the heel |
| **Group 1** | We're gonna polish the toe |
| **Mother Shipton** | I'm gonna sweep the sole |
| **All** | Cockadoodle Doo. |
| **Mother Shipton** | Nick, Stephen, Angela, Sean, Jenny |
| *(calling)* | |

*Group 4 enters*

| **Group 4** | Cockadoodle Doo |
| | It's time to get up, there are jobs to do |
| | We're gonna clean the windows |
| **Group 3** | We're gonna shake the sheets |
| **Group 2** | We're gonna scrub the heel |
| **Group 1** | We're gonna polish the toe |
| **Mother Shipton** | I'm gonna sweep the sole |
| **All** | Cockadoodle Doo. |
| **Mother Shipton** | Simon, Liza, Peter, Eva, Jack |
| *(calling)* | |

*Group 5 enters. Jack is missing*

**Mother Shipton** (*calling*) Jack. Come on; everyone.
**All** (*calling*) Ja—ack.

*Jack, in a nightshirt, enters sleepily*

**Mother Shipton** There you are! What do you think you're doing?
**Jack** Nothing.
**Mother Shipton** Exactly. Nothing. We're all slaving away and you're doing nothing.
**Jack** Sorry, Mother.
**Mother Shipton** *You're* sorry. *I'm* sorry. Idle you are. Bone idle. What are you?
**Jack** (*yawning*) Bone idle.
**Mother Shipton** No, you're not. That's an insult to the average bone. My bones are far from idle. They're at it from dawn to dusk.

*Jack mouths the following speech—he has heard it often before*

Washing, polishing, mending, scrubbing, sweeping, cooking, cleaning, fetching, carrying, sewing, lifting, stretching, bending, tidying, gardening, are you listening?
**Jack** Yes, Mother, your bones are at it from dawn to dusk.

*The Children all join in, smiling*

**Jack** ⎱ Washing, polishing, mending, scrubbing, sweeping, cook- ⎰ *speaking*
            ⎰ ing, cleaning, fetching, carrying, sewing, lifting, stretch- ⎱ *together*
**Children** ⎰ ing, bending...
**Mother Shipton** All right, all right! (*She smiles*) I'm a silly old nag.

*Cocky nods*

What are you nodding for? Do you feel henpecked, too?
**Cocky** (*nodding*) Cockadoodle doo!

|  | SONG 1: (*cont.*) |
|---|---|
| **Group 5** | Cockadoodle Doo |
|  | It's time to get up |
|  | There are jobs to do |
|  | We're gonna light the fire |
| **Group 4** | We're gonna clean the windows |
| **Group 3** | We're gonna shake the sheets |
| **Group 2** | We're gonna scrub the heel |
| **Group 1** | We're gonna polish the toe |
| **Mother Shipton** | I'm gonna sweep the sole |
| **All** | Cockadoodle. |
|  | There was an Old Woman |
| **Mother Shipton** | That's me |
| **All** | Who lived in a shoe |
|  | She had so many children |

| | |
|---|---|
| **Children** | That's us |
| **Mother Shipton** | I didn't know what to |
| | Cockadoodle Doo! |
| **All** | She didn't know what to |
| | Cockadoodle Doo! |
| **Mother Shipton** | There's— |

*Each Child sings his or her own name or Mother Shipton calls the name and each child waves*

*Pause. Mother Shipton realises Jack is missing and goes to the door. She pulls him out by his ear*

There you are! Where have you been this time?
**Jack** Nowhere.
**Mother Shipton** Nowhere. I know where you've been. You've been back to sleep.

*Cocky crows loudly in his ear*

**Cocky** Cockadoodle doo!

*Jack covers his ears and makes a face*

| | |
|---|---|
| **All** (*singing* | And Jack |
| **Group A** | Cockadoodle Doo |
| **Group B** | Cockadoodle Doo |
| **Group A** | Cockadoodle Doo |
| **Group B** | Cockadoodle |
| **All** | Cockadoodle Doo! |

*At the end of the song, all the Children carry on with their jobs. Smoke is seen rising from the chimney. Sheets are being shaken, etc. Cocky approaches Mother Shipton and pecks her on the rear, Mother Shipton swings round and stops sweeping*

**Mother Shipton** Ah! (*Seeing who it is*) Cocky, you cheeky-beaky bird. Stop it!

*Cocky mimes hunger, opening and shutting his mouth/beak*

What? What's the matter? (*She tries to interpret the mime*)

You were kissing me? Didn't feel like a kiss. Oh, you're hungry? You want your breakfast?

*Cocky nods*

Mm. All right.

*She blows a whistle, or bangs her broom to get attention. The Children stop work to listen*

Break-time, everyone.

*Instant pandemonium. The Children cheer and start fighting and playing rowdy games. Mother Shipton gets knocked over in the sudden frenzy of activity. She gets up and is knocked over again. She blows her whistle*

Children, children, please. QUIET!

*The Children listen*

Get ready for breakfast. Jack and Jill, do the honours, please.

*Music. The Children line up. Jack and Jill enter the shoe. Jack emerges with a pile of enamel-type plates or bowls. The Children move speedily in line each taking a plate from the pile. They all end up standing still waiting. Jill returns with a very large packet of cornflakes. The music stops. The Children wait eagerly*

Now wait your turn, everyone, or you'll have to go without.
**Jill** We'll have to go without anyway, Mother. There's hardly any here.

*The Children groan*

**Mother Shipton** Nonsense, dear, there's—(*she takes the packet and looks in it*)—hardly any here, you're right.

*The Children groan again. Mother Shipton puts the packet on the ground and enters the shoe*

There must be another packet ...

*All turn upstage looking at the shoe, waiting for her to return. Tension music as Cocky, unnoticed, struts to the cornflake packet and puts his head inside— eating the contents. Mother Shipton comes back*

Sorry, children, that's all we have; we'll share it out and hunt for some more food this morn ...

*She sees Cocky—head in packet—and stops. The Children see too*

Cocky!

*Cocky straightens, the packet still on his head*

You naughty, naughty bird.

*Mother Shipton removes the packet and shakes it. It is empty. Cocky looks guilty*

That was all the food we had—for the children. How could you?

*Cocky mimes he is sorry*

It's too late to be sorry. You're a foul fowl. (*She is on the verge of tears*) Jack, tie him up with the shoelace; he is not to be trusted.

*Jack leads Cocky off to the "front" of the shoe and ties him to one end of the shoelace. Jill and the others take aside the cornflake packet*

I'm sorry, children.

*The Children gather round her*

I don't know what to do. It's no use pretending. We're overcrowded and underfed and in a mess and up the spout and down the drain and round the twist and—(*she looks up and continues without pause*)—who's that coming?

*Music. They all turn to look off stage*

*The Great Boon enters, pulling or pushing a small caravan with "The Great Boon" written on it. He may even ride a tricycle with the caravan attached. He rings his bell or blows his horn*

**The Great Boon** Aha. Good day. So this is the spot.

**Jack** What?

**The Great Boon** The spot.

**Jack** What spot?

**The Great Boon** Well, I presume that's what you're here for.

**Jack** Sorry?

**The Great Boon** *I'm* sorry. You're a day early.

**Jack** Are we?

**The Great Boon** Yes, it's not till tomorrow.

**Jack** Eh?

**The Great Boon** I've arrived, anyway. Splendid. I thought I was lost.

**Mother Shipton** Not as lost as I am. I haven't understood one word of this conversation. It's all gobbledegook. What isn't till tomorrow?

**The Great Boon** The Circus, madam. The Circus you've come to see.

**Mother Shipton** We haven't come to see a Circus.

**The Great Boon** You haven't come to see a Circus?

**Mother Shipton** No.

**The Great Boon** (*disappointed*) None of you?

**Children** No.

**The Great Boon** Alas, then I *am* lost. Apologies, madam, for the misunderstanding. Tomorrow I perform with the Circus. (*With a change of gear*) Allow me to introduce myself. Ladies and gentlemen, young ladies, young gentlemen, I am The Great Boon, magician extraordinary, presenting magic tricks, instant illusions, major and minor miracles. (*He produces a bunch of flowers*) Madam, for you.

*All clap*

**Mother Shipton** Thank you. I must put them in water.

*Cries of "Encore"*

**The Great Boon** (*enjoying himself*) Please, be seated everyone.

*All sit down to watch the rest of his performance. First there is a drum roll as The Great Boon pulls a long silk handkerchief from his pocket. He shows it back and front, then bunches it up in the way magicians do before producing a dove. Using grand gestures, and with a professional fixed grin, he makes as though to produce a dove, but only succeeds in producing a mini-shower of white feathers*

(*As a swear word*) Abracadabbages. He's flown away again.

*Laughter and applause. The Great Boon now performs a trick that works. This could involve a magical "production" or "disappearance", or could be a stunt defying natural laws: a magical adviser might work with The Great Boon to find one. It should not, however, be too long in performance. At the end of the trick everyone applauds*

Thank you, thank you.

**Mother Shipton** Thank *you*, Mr Great Boon. You've cheered us all up no end.

**The Great Boon** My pleasure, madam.

**Mother Shipton** I'm Mother Shipton, Jack and Jill—my children, and all my adopted children.

**Cocky** Cockadoodle doo!

**Mother Shipton** And Cocky, my adopted cockerel. He's in disgrace.

**The Great Boon** Delighted to make your acquaintances, I'm sure. But, madam, it has not escaped my eagle eye that you and your family live in a somewhat eccentric establishment—

**Mother Shipton** Our shoe? Ah, let me explain. (*To the Children*) Let's *all* explain.

*The Great Boon moves aside to listen to the song*

SONG 2: **The Giant in the Castle**

*The Children act out the story. It is suggested that the "Giant" is played by a child on Jack's shoulders. Jack sings; the child mimes*

| | |
|---|---|
| **Mother Shipton** | Once upon a time, not so long ago |
| | Stood a village on this very spot, though now you'd never know |
| | There were cottages and houses, a Church, a school, a shop |
| | And the families led peaceful lives they thought would never stop. |

| | | |
|---|---|---|
| **Mother Shipton ⎫** **Jill ⎭** | But a giant | ⎧ *Singing* |
| | In a castle | ⎩ *together* |
| | Many miles away | |
| | Said— | |
| **"Giant"** | I want some slaves | |
| | To work for me— | |
| | So I'll search for some today. | |

| | |
|---|---|
| **Mother Shipton** | He said— |
| **"Giant"** | I'll kick all the cottages down |
| | And trample on the trees |
| | I'll worm all the villagers out |
| | And force them to their knees |
| | I'll stuff some in my pocket |
| | The biggest I can see |
| | And carry them back to the castle |
| | Where they can slave for me. |

| | |
|---|---|
| **Mother Shipton** | So he started out on his evil quest |
| | Through the dead of night he lumbered while the village was at rest |

When we heard his footsteps coming, there wasn't time to hide
His enormous legs were cov'ring half a mile with ev'ry stride.

**Mother Shipton** ⎫    And the giant                          ⎧ *Singing*
**Jill**              ⎭    From the castle                        ⎩ *together*
                          Roared an awful roar
                          And our windows smashed
                          We all woke up
                          And our beds jumped from the floor.

**All**                   And then
                          He kicked all the cottages down
                          And trampled on the trees
                          He wormed all the villagers out
                          And forced them to their knees
                          He stuffed some in his pocket
                          The biggest he could see
                          And carried them back to the castle
                          Where slaves they soon would be.

**Mother Shipton**        Somehow I escaped the giant's thieving claws
                          And the kids he must have thought too small to do his
                             dirty chores
                          So he left them sadly crying, their parents torn away
                          Ev'ry building lay in ruins, there was nowhere we could
                             stay.

*The Children accompany the next two verses, singing to "Ah"*

**Mother Shipton** ⎫    Then the giant                          ⎧ *Singing*
**Jill**              ⎭    From the castle                        ⎩ *together*
                          Strode into the night
                          But the children all
                          Refused to let
                          Him escape without a fight.

                          So they chased him
                          And they grabbed him
                          Grabbed him by the shoe
                          And his shoe came off
                          And we moved in
                          'Twas the best that we could do.

**All**                   Because
                          He'd kicked all the cottages down
                          And trampled on the trees
                          He'd wormed all the villagers out
                          And forced them to their knees
                          He'd stuffed some in his pocket
                          The biggest he could see

And carried them back to the castle
Where slaves they soon would be.

So welcome to
Our giant shoe
Where now we live in peace once more
But the price it cost
Was the mums and dads we lost
When the giant waged his war.

When he
Kicked all the cottages down
And trampled on the trees
He wormed all the villagers out
And forced them to their knees
He stuffed some in his pocket
The biggest he could see
And carried them back to the castle
Where slaves they soon would be.

**The Great Boon** What a stirring story. One of the best stories I've ever heard.
And fear not, madam, all good stories have a happy ending.
**Mother Shipton** Well, ours had better come soon or we'll miss it.
**The Great Boon** How do you mean?
**Mother Shipton** We'll have died of starvation first.
**The Children** Mmm, we're starving; we're hungry; mmm, etc.
**Cocky** (*Hungrily*) Cockadoodle doo! (*He comes forward*)

**Mother Shipton** Quiet, Cocky, you're still in disgrace, you're ...

*She notices Cocky is free from the shoelace—one end dangles from his neck.
She picks it up*

Oh no, he's pecked through the shoelace now, as if I didn't have enough
to worry about. (*She removes the bit of shoelace from round his neck*)
**The Great Boon** Allow me. (*He takes it and examines it*)
**Jill** Can we do anything, Mother?
**Mother Shipton** Yes, dear, you and Jack ...

*Jack is not paying attention*

(*Calling*) Jack!

*Jack reacts*

Make yourself useful and go up the hill and fetch a pail of water. Then
at least we can all have a drink. And take Cocky with you before I wring
his neck.
**Jill** Right.
**Jack** 'Bye.

*Jack picks up a pail and exits with Jill. Cocky looks hurt and apologetic, but
follows them*

**The Great Boon** (*calling after them*) If you spot the Circus on your travels, kindly inform it I'm on my way. (*To Mother Shipton*) You see, madam. I have temporarily mislaid the rest of the Circus.

**Mother Shipton** Oh dear, you must think me very rude pestering you with all our problems.

**The Great Boon** Not at all. Allow me to solve (*indicating the shoelace*) at least this one. (*He takes the two severed ends*).

I place the two severed ends in my hands thus and—

*Drum roll*

—after three, we all say the magic words, "Boiled beef and bananas". One, two, three . . .

**All** "Boiled beef and bananas".

**The Great Boon** And, believe it or believe it not, the shoelace is restored! (*He reveals the shoelace back to one piece. For the mechanics of the trick, see note on page viii*)

*All applaud and cheer*

**Child** Can you do any real magic?

**The Great Boon** I beg your pardon?

**Mother Shipton** Lucy, how rude? Please forgive her, Mr Great Boon.

**The Great Boon** Nothing to forgive, madam. I know just what the young lady means. There's magic and magic. I have just demonstrated the magic of skill—but *real* magic with *real* spells—that is something different—and something in which, I fear, my ability is somewhat limited. You see . . .

*As the song starts, all gather to listen. All join in—and sing and dance as the song progresses*

SONG 3: **Two Spells a Day**

(*Singing*)              I'd always loved wizards and sorcerers
                         Like old Merlin at King Arthur's court
                         I bought an old wand

*He produces a wand and waves it—nothing happens*

                         But it wouldn't respond
                         So I found out where I could be taught.

                         I trained at the Magic Academy
                         Where I studied the tricks of the trade
                         The words of each spell—
                         How to chant them as well
                         Till I passed elementary grade.

**Child 1** (*speaking*) What did that mean?

**The Great Boon** It meant I was allowed to do two spells a day.

**Child 2** Only two?

**The Great Boon** Yes.

(*Singing*)                    Just two spells a day
                               Was all I could weave
                               The extent of my magical powers
                               Two spells a day
                               Nothing up my sleeve
                               Two spells ev'ry twenty-four hours.
                               So now I could do minor miracles
                               Change a frog to a prince, change him back
                               Turn water to beer
                               Make a house disappear
                               I was sure I was getting the knack.

**All** (*except The Great Boon*)

                               Just two spells a day
                               Was all he could weave
                               The extent of my magical powers
                               Two spells a day
                               Nothing up his sleeve
                               Two spells ev'ry twenty-four hours.

**The Great Boon**             Three years at the Magic Academy
                               Then my final exams I could take
                               The questions they asked
                               Were the trickiest tasks
                               "Move a mountain" and "dry up a lake".

**Child 3** (*speaking*) You mean if you could move a mountain and dry up a
lake, you'd be allowed more than two spells a day?
**The Great Boon** Exactly. Spells unlimited if I passed the exam.
**Child 4** And if you failed?
**The Great Boon** Doomed to two spells a day—for the rest of my life.
**Child 5** What happened?
**Child 6** Did the lake dry up?
**The Great Boon** (*singing*)
                               Eyes shut I recited the magic words

*He mumbles an unintelligible spell and waves his wand*

                               And the lake slowly started to drain

*All cheer*

                               No water remained—
                               Then it suddenly rained
                               And the lake went and filled up again

*All groan*

                               That didn't impress the examiners
                               But my mountain I moved like a treat
**The Children**               You did it then?

**The Great Boon**      Aaaaaaah...
                        Well I moved it—too far
                        And it squashed the examiners' feet—
*(Speaking)*            I failed.

*(Singing sadly)*       So two spells a day
                        Was all I could weave
                        The extent of my magical powers
                        Two spells a day
                        Nothing up my sleeve
                        Two spells ev'ry twenty-four hours.

**All** (*except The Great Boon*)
                        But
                        With two spells a day
                        You're able to do
                        Almost anything under the sun
                        Two spells a day's
                        Not a lot, it's true—
                        But two spells are better than none.
**The Great Boon**      (*cheering up*)
                        You're right!
**All**                 Two spells are better than none!

*All applaud*

**The Great Boon** Thank you, my friends, thank you. Well, I must be off. The Circus calls. Though I wish it would call a little louder; then I might find it.

**Mother Shipton** Good luck, Mr Great Boon.

**The Great Boon** Thank you, madam. It's been a pleasure. (*He produces another bunch of flowers for her*) For you.

**Mother Shipton** How kind. I must put them in water.

**The Great Boon** Farewell, friends.

*The Great Boon and his caravan start to exit*

**Children** 'Bye, cheerio, etc.

*All wave. Suddenly the atmosphere changes dramatically. Loud thudding giant footsteps are heard, and huge shadows are cast over the set. A menacing, loud cackle is heard over speakers. The Great Boon stops. All react bewildered.*

**The Great Boon** Heavens! What's going on?

*All look around nervously as the noise gets louder. Suddenly a child looks up and off, then screams violently*

**Child** Look. Look! (*She points off*)

*All look and react horrified. The Children scream and run for cover behind the shoe. Mother Shipton reacts terrified on the spot*

**The Great Boon** What is it, madam?

**Mother Shipton** L-l-l-look, the G-G-G-Giant!

*They cower in fright*


SONG 4: **Where's My Shoe?**
*During the song, the Giant's voice and footsteps should suggest he is getting nearer and nearer*
**Giant** (*singing off*) Shoe, shoe
                        Where's my shoe?
                        Shoe, shoe
                        Where are you?
                        Shoe, shoe
                        My foot is bare
                        Where's my shoe?

**Mother Shipton** (*Cowering behind the Great Boon*) He wants his shoe back. Our lovely home.

*The Children help her as she rushes to the shoe and tries to push it off out of sight. It will not budge. The footsteps continue and maybe odd loud grunts from the Giant. Exciting shadows swing all over the stage. Suddenly a very loud alarm bell goes off—eclipsing all other noises. All stop their activity to listen, confused. The Great Boon, with a big gesture, takes an oversize alarm clock from a pocket in his cloak. Mother Shipton jumps violently*

Aaaaaah! Fire! Fire! Fire! (*She starts rushing round and getting nowhere*)
**The Great Boon** No, madam, this bell means I can do a real magic spell.
**Mother Shipton** What, now?
**The Great Boon** Yes. Twelve hours have elapsed since the last one.
**Mother Shipton** Well, don't just stand there, Mr Great Boon. Magic that great fat Giant away.
**The Great Boon** Yes, of course. Er—here goes. (*He takes up his magician's pose, and waves his wand*)
Jiggery, pokery, oink, ink, ink,
Pokery, jiggery, shrink, shrink, SHRINK.
*There is a huge flash, then the lights black-out. Noise covers the transformation. When the Lights come up, the shoe has gone. Also the Giant's noises have stopped. And no shadows are cast on the set. At first, Mother Shipton, The Great Boon and the Children do not notice that the shoe has disappeared. They are looking off where the Giant was. All cheer*

**Child 1** The Giant's gone!
**Child 2** The magic worked!
**Child 3** Well done, Mr Great Boon!

*Cheers*

**Mother Shipton** How can we ever thank you?
**The Great Boon** My pleasure, madam.
**Mother Shipton** You've saved us all. And our lovely home ... (*She turns her*

*head towards it, then back to The Great Boon).* We're very grate ... (*She stops, then does a huge double-take*) It's gone! It's gone!

*The Children notice now and rush to where it was. The Great Boon turns, and realizes too*

**The Great Boon** (*with a gasp*) Abracadabbages! You know what's happened?
**Mother Shipton** Our home's disappeared, that's what's happened. Why?
**The Great Boon** Because when I magicked away the Giant, I automatically magicked away his shoe too. Apologies, madam, apologies.

*One of the children finds something*

**Child** (*bringing something forward*) Look at this.

*All cluster round and look—it is a human-size shoe—a miniature version of their home*

**Another Child** It's our home.
**The Great Boon** Abracadabbages! Well I'm blowed. My spell couldn't have been powerful enough to make the Giant's shoe disappear altogether. It just reduced it to a human-size shoe. Amazing.
**Mother Shipton** Amazing it may be, but amazingly inconvenient too. We can't live in there!
**Child** What about the Giant?
**The Great Boon** What about him?
**Child** Well, if your spell magicked the *shoe* down to human size ...
**The Great Boon** (*his eyes widening with the realization*) ... it must have magicked the Giant down to human size too.
**Mother Shipton** You mean you didn't make him disappear?

*Dramatic chord. The Great Boon shakes his head*

**The Great Boon** Somewhere near lurks a human-sized Giant, and I hardly think he's in a friendly mood.

*The Children eye each other nervously*

**Mother Shipton** Come on children, let's hide in the wood for a while. Oh dear.

SONG 4A: **Cockadoodle Doo/There Was an Old Woman** (*reprise*)

*As they sing, they start to exit, accompanied by Mother Shipton and the Great Boon*

**All**     Cockadoodle Doo
         There was an old woman who lost a shoe
         So now what is she to
         Cockadoodle—Doo?

*All exit*

*The scene quickly changes to a traditional-style water well on a hill or mound. Beside it is an apple tree, which has seen better days*

*The Giant enters. He is human-size but if possible should be very tall so that he is still a menacing character rather than a weak one. He carries a club.*

*One of his shoes is missing—he walks with one bare foot. He reels uncertainly—following his shrinking. He still speaks in deliberate low tones*

**Giant** (*clutching his forehead*) Ohhhhh! I'm gizzy and diddy—dizzy and giddy. (*To himself, not the audience*) What's happened? (*He staggers towards the well, and peers through his blurred eyes.*) Ah, my castle—go and lie down. (*He reaches the well*) It's not my castle! Where am I? (*He looks around and up and down*) Ahhhh! I've shrunk! I've shrivelled! Grrrrrr! (*He rants and raves waving his club*) Calm down. Got to work out what to do. (*He thinks*) Must be dreaming, that's it. Close eyes and pinch myself to wake up. (*He closes eyes and pinches himself*) Aaaaaaah! I'm not dreaming. (*He sees water in the well*). Water! Feel better after a drink. (*He scoops some up and drinks*) Hungry too. Haven't been eating too well—(*idea*)—maybe that's why I've shrunk. (*He sees some apples on the ground*) What are these? Cherries? (*He bites*) Apples. (*He spits out*) Ugh! *Rotten* apples. (*He cries*) Food, I need FOOD!

**Cocky** (*off*) Cockadoodle doo!
**Jill** (*off, more distant*) Hurry up Jack, nearly there.
**Jack** (*off, more distant still*) Coming!
*The Giant reacts to the voice, and hides behind the well*
*Cocky enters, clucking and strutting. He looks over his "shoulder" and clucks to the others, off stage, to hurry up*

*The Giant, at this moment, emerges from hiding and looks eagerly at Cocky*

Food, food!

*Cocky turns back, making the Giant recoil and hide again. He struts towards the well. He doesn't notice the Giant creep round from behind the well, tiptoeing, club held aloft. He advances menacingly on Cocky. Tension music. The audience may shout a warning to Cocky. In any event he senses something is wrong and struts away from the well, followed by the creeping Giant. If the audience is shouting, Cocky tries to understand them. In any event he suddenly does a fowl-like right angle turn just as the Giant strikes with the club. The Giant falls over, missing Cocky. Cocky has not noticed. The Giant shakes his fists with frustration. He follows Cocky to the other side. Cocky is still suspicious, and/or following the audience—trying to understand them. Again the Giant slams down the club just as Cocky turns. As the club misses its quarry, the Giant falls to the ground and beats the ground in fury. Cocky struts on*

**Jill** (*off*) Here we are.
*The Giant reacts and dashes back to hide behind the well*
*Jill enters, dragging a breathless Jack. Jack carries the pail*
*Music as Jack and Jill climb the hill to fetch a pail of water—the nursery rhyme theme is the obvious choice of tune. Cocky struts about below. Jill, being the practical one, goes to sort out the winding mechanism. Jack stands with the pail. Suddenly the Giant—clubless—emerges smiling charmingly, and stands right behind Jack*
*The next section should be played with great pace; otherwise the audience may try to warn Jack and Jill that this is the Giant*

**Giant** How much?

*Jack turns and jumps violently—the Giant has taken him by surprise and is much taller than he.*

**Jack** What?

**Giant** How much—do you want for it? (*He looks at Cocky*).

**Jack** How much do I want for it? (*He looks at the pail*) Well, it's not worth much, it's a bit rusty...

**Giant** (*booming*) Not that! (*Correcting himself to his former charming self*) No, no, no!

**Jack** No, no, no?

**Giant** No, no, no, no, no!

**Jack** No, no, no, no, no?

**Giant** (*booming*) No!

*Jacks jumps. The Giant smiles again. Jill becomes aware of the conversation: she joins in*

**Jill** What's going on? (*To the Giant*) Who are you?

**Giant** (*bowing low—a bit too unctuously*) Dear little lady.

**Jack** You don't look like a dear little lady to me.

**Jill** Shut up, Jack.

**Giant** I was merely enquiring of young—er, Jack?— how much you might be wanting—for that bird.

**Jill** Cocky? Nothing.

**Giant** (*surprised*) Nothing?

**Jill** He's not for sale.

**Giant** No?

**Jill** No.

**Jack** No.

**Giant** Oh.

**Jill** Not oh. No!

**Jack** Oh no!

**Giant** I could offer you—(*thinking frantically*)—all these—juicy apples. (*He produces the apples from his pocket, takes the pail from Jack and starts putting the apples in, as many as possible*)

**Jill** Sorry.

**Jack** (*eyeing the apples*) Jill. (*He takes her to one side*)

*Cocky listens*

I think we should say yes.

**Jill** Why?

**Jack** Well, all the children are starving. Mother's always telling me to be useful—she'd be pleased if I took back some food for every one.

**Jill** But we can't. Cocky's our pet.

**Jack** Listen. Only this morning Mother said she could wring Cocky's neck.

**Jill** But even so...

**Jack** All he does is wake us all up too early, peck through shoelaces and eat our cornflakes. I like him, but the children come first.

**Jill** Yes, but—I don't like the look of that man. (*Raising her voice*) I think we ought to get back to the shoe.
**Giant** (*overhearing*) Shoe? What shoe?
**Jill** We live in a shoe—a giant's shoe.
**Giant** Really?
**Jack** I'm going to do it.
**Jill** Jack.

*She tries to stop Jack, but in vain. Jack returns to the Giant*

**Jack** All right. Cocky's yours.

*Cocky reacts, clucking*

Go on, Cocky, off you go with the nice gentleman.

*Cocky pulls away, but Jack leads him to the Giant*

**Giant** Come along, Cocky, I won't hurt you. (*He hands over the pail, and takes a rope from round his waist. He ties Cocky by the neck.*)
**Jill** (*distraught*) I'm sorry, Cocky, I didn't want to...

*Music. Cocky runs to Jill, who kisses him goodbye. The Giant, holding onto the rope, goes and finds his club. He emerges—a different character now he has had his way*

**Giant** Come here, you mangy fowl, you're mine now.

*He wields the club and uses it to force Cocky to move on ahead "down the hill". Jill, upset, looks on, appalled*

**Jill** Jack, how *could* we?
**Jack** Mother will be very pleased with us. (*He bites an apple happily.*) Ugh. (*He pulls a face*)
**Jill** What?
**Jack** (*unable to believe it*) It's rotten! (*He looks in the pail*) They *all* are.

*Jill takes the apple and puts two and two together*

**Jill** Hey! Stop.

*The Giant turns*

These apples are rotten. *You're* rotten. A rotten cheat.
**Giant** You're too late—(*Sneering*)—dear little lady.
**Jack** (*putting the pail down and approaching bravely*) Give us Cocky back!
**Giant** Grrrrrrrh!

*The Giant brandishes his club. Jack ducks to avoid being hit, and falls down the hill*

**Jill** (*furiously stamping on the Giant's bare foot*) You...
**Giant** Aaaaaaaaaah!

*The Giant threatens Jill with the club; she recoils, and falls down the hill too— thus fulfilling the demands of the nursery rhyme*

Ha, ha, ha, ha, ha.

*Laughing maniacally, the Giant starts to exit, dragging Cocky on the rope. Jill jumps up and chases the Giant*

**Jill** Look, it's rotten! (*She shoves the apple in his face*)
**Giant** That's *your* prob ... (*He stops and starts to tremble*) Ah—ah—w-w-w-what's th-th-th-that? (*He points to the apple*)

**Jill** (*looking*) It's a sort of maggot—caterpillar—I told you, the apple's *rotten.*
**Giant** (*almost uncontrollable*) M-m-maggot? C-c-c-caterpillar—(*He shrieks*) —it's a crawly creepy—a creepy crawly. Ugh. (*He gives a huge shudder, knees knocking*). Ah, ah, ahhhhhhhhhhh!

*Screaming, the Giant exits, dragging Cocky after him*

*Jill goes to chase after him. Then, realizing she could never catch him, she looks back at Jack, who is rubbing his head from his fall*

**Jack** (*feeling very guilty*) Sorry, Jill.
**Jill** Too late for being sorry.
**Jack** I didn't know he was a baddie!
**Jill** I think he was more than a baddie. Didn't you notice? He had a shoe missing...

*Dramatic chord. They look at each other, confused but suspicious. Then they exit towards home, maybe through the auditorium, carrying the pail of apples, and yelling "Mother, Mother"*

*Music covers the scene change back to the original setting. This should be very quick, covered partially by Jack and Jill's journey round the auditorium.*

*When the scene change is complete, Mother Shipton enters, summoned by the cries of "Mother, Mother". She carries the shoe. The Great Boon follows her on, leaving his caravan visible, but out of the way of the action. Possibly one or two Children peer round the proscenium arch or the side of the set. Jack and Jill arrive breathlessly*

**Mother Shipton** Hallo, dears, welcome home.
**Jill** Mother, listen...
**Jack** We've just met...
**Mother Shipton** (*taking the pail from Jack*) Well done, both of you. The children are all very thirsty. (*She moves towards The Great Boon*)
**Jill** Mother, please, listen...
**Jack** You don't understand.....
**Mother Shipton** (*to The Great Boon*) What a reliable pair—what a help— what—(*she suddenly looks in the pail and notices what's inside*)—on earth are these?
**Jack** (*embarrassed*) Rotten apples.
**Jill** We're trying to exp...
**Mother Shipton** Rotten apples? Where's the water?
**Jack** (*lamely*) We forgot it.

**Mother Shipton** (*imitating him*) "We forgot it". You forgot the water and got rotten apples instead. I give up.

**Jill** But, Mother, we met this man...

**Mother Shipton** Man, what man? And where's Cocky?

*Silence*

I said, where's Cocky?

**Jack** (*quietly*) I swapped him for the rotten apples. The man suggested it and I thought we needed food and you'd said you could wring Cocky's neck and I wanted to be useful and—I'm sorry. (*He is close to tears*)

*Mother Shipton starts to speak, then thinks better of it. She blinks back a tear*

**Mother Shipton** Cocky. I raised him from an egg.

**Jill** (*wide-eyed suddenly noticing something is missing*) Hey, I've just noticed—where's the shoe?

*Mother Shipton holds out the human-sized shoe*

**The Great Boon** I'm responsible, I fear. The Giant came in search of it, I tried to magic him away, but only succeeded in cutting him down to human size. And his shoe unfortunately.

**Jill** It was him!

**The Great Boon** I beg your pardon?

**Jill** He was the man we met.

**Mother Shipton** (*coming out of her sad reverie*) What?

**Jack** (*realizing*) He's got Cocky.

**Jill** He had a shoe missing...

**Jack** And a club—he tried to hit us.

**Mother Shipton** Cocky's with the Giant?

*Jack and Jill nod*

Oh, I don't know. How could you do such a thing? I just don't know what I am going to do? (*She sobs*) Throw these rotten apples away for a start.

*A very loud bell rings. All jump*

**Jill** What's that?

**Mother Shipton** (*throwing the apples away—off one side of the stage—and mouthing over the noise of the bell*) The Great Boon's alarm clock.

*All the children enter drawn by the noise*

*The Great Boon manages to stop the ringing*

**Children** (*all together, excitedly*) Can we have another spell, now? Time for another one? Please, Mr Great Boon! etc.

**The Great Boon** Very well. Another spell!

*Cheers*

What's it to be?

**Jack** Could you bring Cocky back? (*To the Children*) The Giant's got Cocky.

*The Children react*

Could you magic him back?
**The Great Boon** Certainly. (*He takes up a pose*)
**Mother Shipton** No, wait, Mr Great Boon. Much as I love Cocky and want
  him back, the children come first. Let's get our home back please. Stand
  back, children. (*She makes a space and sets down the shoe.*)
**The Great Boon** As you wish, madam. (*With a chuckle*) Or rather, as I wish.
  (*He takes up pose—silence. Then he stops.*) Abracadabbages, I've just
  thought—such a reverse spell will also enlarge the Giant again. Is that wise?
  With him so near?
**Mother Shipton** I hadn't thought of that.
**The Great Boon** Why not wait till morning when he may be farther away?
**Jill** He's right, Mother.
**The Great Boon** If I might suggest—the children are hungry—perhaps I can
  create some food?
**Mother Shipton** Good idea, Mr Great Boon, go ahead.
**The Great Boon** Thank you, madam. (*He takes up pose and waves his wand*)

Jiggery, pokery
Yummy, yum yum
Pokery jiggery
For tummy, tum tum.

*Flash. Blackout. Music. The Lights come up on one side of the stage as a magical
apple tree starts to grow—half off, half on stage*

**Jack** What's happening?
**Jill** It's the rotten apples—look!
**Jack** They're not so rotten after all!

SONG 5: **Grow**
*During the song the tree continues to grow. Big apples are visible. The Children
watch and join in the song*

| | |
|---|---|
| **The Great Boon** | Can you believe the impossible? |
| (*singing*) | Can you believe what you see? |
| | The apples are growing |
| **All** | And growing |
| | And growing |
| **The Great Boon** | Into a magical tree. |
| | See it |
| | Grow and grow |
| | Grow and grow |
| | Grow and grow |
| | The craziest sight |
| | You ever did see |
| **All** | See it |
| | Grow and grow |
| | Grow and grow |

Grow and grow and grow and grow—a magic tree!
See it climb so high
Sure it's gonna touch the sky.
See it
Grow and grow
It's unbelievable
Grow and grow
It's inconceivable
Grow and grow
Way up through the clouds
Way up in the blue
See it
Grow and grow
It's growing quicker and
Grow and grow
It's growing thicker and
Grow and grow and grow and grow—it can't be true!

**The Great Boon** It's incredible
All the fruit is edible

**All** Grow and grow,
Grow and grow,
Grow and grow.

**The Great Boon** It's unbeatable
All the fruit is eatable!

**All** See it
Grow and grow (*clap,clap,clap*)
Grow and grow (*clap,clap,clap*)
Grow and grow (*clap,clap,clap*)
Grow and grow (*clap,clap,clap*)
Grow and grow (*clap,clap,clap*)
Grow and grow (*clap,clap,clap*)
Grow and grow and grow and grow and grow
See it
Grow and grow
Ooooooooooh!
Grow and grow
Ooooooooooh!
Grow and grow
The craziest sight
You ever did see
See it
Grow and grow
Ooooooooooh!
Grow and grow
Ooooooooooh!
Grow and grow and grow and grow—a magic tree!

See it
Grow and grow
Higher, higher, higher
Grow and grow
Higher, higher, higher
Grow and grow
Way up through the clouds
Way up in the blue
See it
Grow and grow
Higher, higher, higher
Grow and grow
Higher, higher, higher
Grow and grow and grow and grow—it can't be true!
Grow and grow and grow and grow and grow
Grow and grow and grow and grow and grow and grow
It can't be true!

*At the end of the song, all cheer. The Children run to the tree and pick apples—
possibly helped by Jack and Jill. The Lights now suggests dusk*

**Mother Shipton** Just one each, children. Don't push. Thank you, Mr Great
Boon.
**The Great Boon** My privilege, madam.
**Mother Shipton** You will stay with us till morning?
**The Great Boon** Of course. In twelve hours time I'll magic your home back,
and then I must set off in search of the circus. We perform tomorrow,
you know. Good night.

*The Lights continue to go down*

**Mother Shipton** Sleep well. Come on, children, sheets. We're sleeping rough
tonight.

*The Children fetch the sheets from where they left them earlier. All huddle round
Mother Shipton*

*The Great Boon goes off to his caravan*

*The shoe is left on the ground in full view of the audience*

**Jack** I'm sorry about Cocky, Mother.
**Mother Shipton** So am I, dear. But he's a wily old bird. I don't think we've
seen the last of him. Let's hope not anyway.
**Jill** 'Night, Mother.
**Children** 'Night, Mother.
**Mother Shipton** 'Night, children. God bless. And God bless your mums and
dads in the castle. And Cocky.

SONG 6: **Till Today Becomes Tomorrow**

*During the song, the moon and stars perhaps become visible*

**Mother Shipton**          Moon shine brightly through the darkness up above
(*singing*) *or* **Jill**   Stars shine down on us and ev'ryone we love
                            May your warm and friendly light
                            See us safely through the night
                            Till the breaking of a brand new dawn
                            Tomorrow.

                            Till today becomes tomorrow
                            Keep on shining
                            Till today becomes tomorrow
                            Light up the sky
                            Your reassuring glow
                            Will keep us from harm we know
                            Till today becomes tomorrow
                            By and by.

**All**                     Moon shine brightly through the darkness up above
                            Stars shine down on us and ev'ryone we love
                            May your warm and friendly light
                            See us safely through the night
                            Till the breaking of a brand new dawn
                            Tomorrow.

                            Till today becomes tomorrow
                            Keep on shining
                            Till today becomes tomorrow
                            Light up the sky
                            Your reassuring glow
                            Will keep us from harm we know
                            Till today becomes tomorrow
                            By and by.

                            Till today becomes tomorrow
                            Keep on shining
                            Till today becomes tomorrow
                            Light up the sky
                            Your reassuring glow
                            Will keep us from harm we know
                            Till today becomes tomorrow
                            By and by
                            Till today becomes tomorrow
                            By and by.

*After the song, with a few "Good Nights", all settle down to sleep*

*Time-lapse music. The Lights slowly suggest the passing of time—night through
to dawn—nearly twelve hours*

*All are still asleep*

*The Giant enters stealthily, pulling on the rope which is tied round Cocky's neck. Sinister music*

**Giant** Come on, you miserable bird, where is it? Where's my shoe?

*Cocky is reluctant to tell him: he pulls away, shaking his head. Suddenly the Giant spots the shoe in front of all the sleeping people*

There it is!

*Tension music, as the Giant creeps softly towards the shoe. Cocky sees the Giant is going to get it unless he does something. He has an idea, and in the nick of time puffs out his chest and crows*

**Cocky** (*very loudly*) Cockadoodle doo! Cockadoodle doo!

*The Giant turns, taken by surprise. All wake up*

**Jill** It's the Giant!
**Jack** Get him!

*Music, as the Children charge towards the Giant. He starts lashing out with his club, trying to force his way through. He drops Cocky's rope. How complicated the chase is will depend upon individual directors—it could, for instance, use the auditorium as well as the stage. At any event, in this first part, the Giant manages to huff and puff and club his way through the Children, who all bob back up again like resilient corks. Maybe some of the smaller children climb on the backs of the larger ones, like jockeys, for extra height in the attack. Maybe some crouch down to trip up the Giant*

*Eventually the Giant escapes off followed by the Children*

*Cocky and Mother Shipton, who have separately been caught up in the whirl of activity, are now reunited. Mother Shipton hugs Cocky. But not for long*

*The chase comes back, the Giant running from the Children. He sees Mother Shipton and Cocky ahead of him and chases them off the other side, L. A second or two later the children come chasing on R after the Giant. They too exit L, whooping with excitement*

*At this point the music is interrupted by a very loud alarm bell—the Great Boon's clock*

*The Great Boon enters, sleepy but excited, from his caravan. He is semi-dressed—minus his cloak and jacket. He carries the alarm clock*

**The Great Boon** Time to magic Mother Shipton's shoe back to size! (*He sees it on the ground*) There it is! (*He notices the empty area; speaks to himself, not to the audience*) Where is everyone? Never mind, I'll do it as a surprise for them. Just get prepared.

*The Great Boon returns to his caravan and enters it, just as Cocky and Mother Shipton enter L, on the run. The chase music starts again. Mother Shipton is exhausted and breathless. She stops C to recover. Cocky tries fanning her with his wing's. He anxiously looks behind him, then turns back Immediately, the Giant enters L at speed; he grabs Cocky by the rope again and drags him off R*

*Mother Shipton reacts and starts wearily after them*

*Jack and Jill, followed by the Children, dash on L.*

*Mother Shipton points off R.*

*Jack, Jill and the Children dash off R. Mother Shipton limps after them. The Great Boon immediately enters from the caravan, looking immaculate. He is, of course, totally unaware of the chase in progress. He checks the position of the shoe, then takes up a pose*

*Drum roll. The Great Boon stops posing*

Silly old Boon. Forgotten my magic wand.

*The Great Boon returns inside the caravan*

*The music starts again*

*The Giant and Cocky immediately enter R, breathless*

*The Giant looks wildly about and finds a spot to hide—ideally near the magic tree, or behind the caravan. He need not be out of sight of the audience, but when the others enter chasing across the stage, they do not see him*

*Jack, Jill and the Children enter R, go past the Giant and start to exit L*

*Before Jack and Jill are out of sight, the Giant and Cocky emerge from hiding and start to go off R*

*Mother Shipton enters R and takes the Giant by surprise*

*Mother Shipton puts her fingers to her mouth and gives a loud whistle—possibly done over offstage speakers. The Children, with Jack and Jill, turn, see the Giant, and start back. Feeling cornered, the Giant takes the only course available to him—upwards—pushing Cocky ahead. They both climb the magic tree. Ideally, after a few upward steps they both disappear from view, as if climbing the offstage part of the tree. Jack, Jill and the Children arrive at the foot of the tree. Tension music*

**Mother Shipton** He's up the magic tree!
**Jack** If only I had an axe—I could chop the tree down and be Jack the Giant-killer.
**Mother Shipton** I'm having no heroics, dear. Anyway, Cocky's up there too. He's suffered enough.
**Jill** And if he hadn't woken us up, anything could have happened.

*All look up the tree*

*The Great Boon enters from his caravan. He walks to his spell-uttering position, he sees the others, and smiles in anticipation*

**The Great Boon** There you are. Good morning. (*He quickly takes up his pose.*)
**All** Good morning, Mr Great Boon.
**The Great Boon** (*waving his wand*) Pokery, jiggery, po ho ho.
**Mother Shipton** What's he doing?
**The Great Boon** Jiggery, pokery, grow, grow, GROW.
**Jill** Stop, stop!

*Jill is too late. Flash, black-out, music. When the Lights go up again, the shoe
is back to its original size*

*If it is not too dangerous, some of the Children could be discovered on top of
the shoe, as if they were standing near it as it grew and were carried upwards
by its growth! This could be achieved by keeping a few Children off stage during
the last chase across, and pre-setting them on the shoe waiting to come on in
the black-out*

*The Great Boon bows*

**The Great Boon** Madam—your home!

*Mother Shipton comes forward, her concern for what is happening up the tree
temporarily eclipsed by her pleasure at seeing her home again. The Children clap
and cheer*

**Mother Shipton** Oh, thank you, Mr Great Boon, what a relief. (*She opens
  the door, delighted*)
**The Great Boon** My pleasure. Well, I must search for the Circus once more,
  now your problems are over.....

*The Giant's voice is heard very loud and booming, from speakers, if possible,
overhead. At first he sounds confused, then realizes that he has grown again,
and is filled with delight*

**Giant** Huh? Huh? Oh! (*Realizing*) Ah! Ha, hahaha ha!

*All turn in fright towards the magic tree and look upwards; they realize that
the Giant has been affected by the magic too*

**Jill** Something tells me our problems are only just beginning. (*To the Great
  Boon*) You've magicked the Giant back to size as well.

*The Great Boon reacts worried*


SONG 6A: **Where's my Shoe?** (*reprise*)

*During the song, all react frightened, looking up. After a couple of lines, a terri-
fied Cocky manages to descend the tree, helped by Jack and Jill. He is reconci-
led with Mother Shipton. Then in the last couple of lines, as though the Giant is
climbing down the tree, a Giant bare foot descends from the flies*

**Giant** (*off*)    Shoe, shoe
                 Where's my shoe?
                 Shoe, shoe
                 Where are you?

Shoe, shoe
My foot is bare
Where's my shoe?

*The foot is poised for further descent. Pandemonium; Children screaming and hiding behind the shoe, hustled away by Mother Shipton. Booming laughter from the Giant, as*

*the* CURTAIN *falls*

# ACT II

*As the Lights go down we hear grunts and threatening noises from the Giant over the speakers. These disappear as the Curtain rises and we see the shoe area only lit. Mother Shipton, The Great Boon, Cocky, Jack and Jill and the Children are grouped on and around the shoe. They sing an opening song almost as a tableau comment—in other words the action has momentarily stopped*

SONG 6B: **Cockadoodle Doo/There was an Old Woman** (*reprise*)

**All**    Cockadoodle Doo
There was an old woman who found a shoe
But she found a giant too!
So now what are we to
Cockadoodle—Doo?

*At the end of the short song, the Lights come back on—to suggest morning again. The action takes up virtually where it left off at the end of Act I. The Giant, barefoot, is still visible as though climbing down. Everyone round the shoe looks up with horror. The Giant grunts through the speakers*

**Jack**  He's coming down!

*The Children react. Cocky clucks*

**Mother Shipton**  Now keep calm, everyone. It's all right. (*She is far from calm*)
Keep calm. Don't panic. Don't panic. (*She moves agitatedly*)

*The Giant grunts*

He—lp!

*Jack and Jill hold on to her*

**Jill**  Shh, Mother. He'll hear us.
**The Great Boon**  Hardly. He's so huge, his ears must be up amongst the clouds.

*The Giant grunts. All react. The foot lifts up and disappears*

**Jack**  He's climbing up again!
**Jill**  No. He couldn't get a good footing.
**Mother Shipton**  I'll give him a good footing! (*She mimes a kick*)

*The Giant grunts. The tree shakes and creaks with the weight*

**Jill**  He's climbing down the other side.

*Their eyes follow his descent off stage. His shoe-clad foot reaches the ground with a hard thud*

**Jack** Foot one. With shoe.

*The bare foot reaches the ground with a soft thud*

Foot two. Without shoe.

*Slow footsteps start, one heavy, one light. If possible, they are stereophonic and make the Giant appear to be walking across the Auditorium—R to L. All heads follow his progress. Maybe he casts huge shadows over the stage. He reaches, as it were, off L. As he goes he gives the odd grunt*

He's going!

**Mother Shipton** Thank goodness.

*Suddenly there's a huge crash. All react*

**Giant** (*off*) Ohhhhh! (*He moans in pain*)

**Mother Shipton** (*looking off* L) Look. He's fallen over. He must have stubbed his toe—he's rubbing it.

**The Great Boon** Bound to happen if you're stupid enough to walk barefoot in a forest!

**Giant** (*off*) Ooooooh! My toe! I must find my shoe. Now, where did I see it?

*All look around fearfully. The odd grunt from the Giant continues at a discreet volume during the following lines*

**Mother Shipton** He's going to find it, I know he is! Our lovely house! What are we going to do?

**The Great Boon** Apologies, madam. I cannot help—(*he looks at his clock*)—for another eleven hours fourteen minutes and fifty-two seconds.

*Suddenly Cocky steps away from the shoe, gets their attention, and acts tired and sleepy*

Cocky, this isn't the time for a snooze. Wake up.

*Cocky clucks and shakes his head, trying to make them understand. He indicates offstage, then covers his eyes*

**Jill** Hey, Mother. He's not going to sleep—he's saying if the Giant were asleep—

**The Great Boon** (*realizing*) —he wouldn't see the shoe. Abracadabbages, he's right.

**Mother Shipton** But the Giant isn't asleep. He's wide awake, rubbing his big toe.

**Jack** We'll *send* him to sleep. Well done, Cocky—I'm sorry I ever said you were useless.

**Jill** He's cleverer than any of us.

**Mother Shipton** I'm sorry. I still don't understand. *How* do we send this Giant to sleep?

**Jack** Cocky?

*Cocky sort of sings in a clucking voice*

**Jill** Sing to him, of course. We'll sing him a lullaby. Come on, everyone—the one Mother sings to us, 'Hushabye Children'—only *we'll* sing 'Hushabye Giant'.

SONG 7: **Hushabye Giant**
*During the song, the children all do the actions in between the lines*

**All**     Hushabye Giant
            Close your eyes

*Yawn and stretch*

            Sleep tight

*Zzzzzzz*

            Hushabye Giant
            Sweet dreams

*Snore/Whistle*

            Good night.

*At the end of the song, all look off expectantly. The Giant grunts, then sings unaccompanied*

**Giant** (*off*)     Shoe shoe,
                      Where's my shoe . . .
**Mother Shipton** It's no use, he can't hear us. Maybe he's deaf.
**The Great Boon** No, no, no, madam, as I pointed out previously, he's so vast, his ears are too far distant to pick up the sound waves of our voices. It needs to be louder.
**Jack** Louder? I can't sing any louder.
**Children** Nor can I; we'd never sing loud enough; etc.

*Suddenly Cocky clucks and flaps his wings, indicating the audience*

**Mother Shipton** Cocky, quiet! What is it now? (*She suddenly sees the audience*) Oo-er! Look.

*All look at the audience, amazed*

**Jack** People.
**Jill** Sitting.
**Mother Shipton** Waiting for something to happen!
**The Great Boon** Abracadabbages, of course! (*Confidentially*) They've come to see the Circus.
**Mother Shipton** What Circus?
**The Great Boon** The Circus I've been looking for.

*Cocky indicates the audience and makes singing clucking noises*

**Jill** Maybe they'd help us. Join in. That would make the lullaby louder and the Giant might hear it.
**The Great Boon** Splendid idea. I'll ask them. (*He edges forward to the audience*)

Ladies and gentlemen, young ladies, young gentlemen. I apologize for the delay. The Circus will commence as soon as possible. Meanwhile we, er, have a little problem; in fact it's rather a large problem. The point is—would you help us try to sing the Giant to sleep? Would you?

*Audience participation*

Not too loud, the Giant might hear you too soon! Would you? Oh, thank you.

*He returns to the others, who smile thankfully at the audience*

Perhaps we could organize some words for them.

*Rather than use a song-sheet, which, in this tense situation, could destroy any sense of reality—"we just happen to have the words written down"—it is suggested that the Children pick up pieces of "chalk" and appear to write the words, one word per child, on the boot itself, or on the sheets—which could be pre-prepared with the writing on—or on clothes which are swiftly pegged to the shoelace like a clothes line. This should not turn into a production number—but an apparently improvized way of displaying the words is preferable to the illogical immediate display of a specially prepared song-sheet. Alternatively, the Great Boon could produce the words from a hat—silk handkerchiefs, say, each with a word written on, which can then be held up by the Children*

Jack and Jill, you could conduct.

**Jack** All right.

**Jill** Here goes.

**Jack** ⎫
**Jill** ⎭ One, two, three.            ⎧ *Speaking*
                                      ⎩ *together*

*All sing the song again, leading the audience, and encouraging them to do the actions too*

**All**     Hushabye Giant
            Close your eyes

*Yawn and stretch*

            Sleep tight

*Zzzzzzzz*

            Hushabye Giant
            Sweet dreams

*Snore/Whistle*

            Good night.

**Jill** Lovely!

*All look off expectantly*

**Giant** (*off, with a huge yawn*) Now—where's—my—shoe?

*There is a sound of snoring—Mother Shipton is asleep*

**Jack** You've nodded Mother off, anyway. Mother! (*He wakes her up*).
**Mother Shipton** Sorry, dear. What happened?
**Jill** Nearly there. Thanks everybody. Once more and we've got him! One, two, three.

*They lead the audience again*

**All**    Hushabye Giant
           Close your eyes

*Yawn and stretch*

           Sleep tight

*Zzzzzzzz*

           Hushabye Giant
           Sweet dreams

*Snore/Whistle*

           Good night.

*Everyone looks off. Tension music. The Giant yawns again, then he can be heard stretching, before lying down to go to sleep. As he stretches, Mother and the others watch, and back away from a huge giant matching boot, the upturned heel of which enters—i.e. the Giant is lying on his back, parallel with the audience, in a straight line offstage; when he stretches, his upturned foot appears. Then a second foot enters, below the first; this is the bare foot. Loud, deep, contented snores are heard from the Giant*

**Mother Shipton** Well done, everybody, thank you!
**The Great Boon** (*concerned*) Oh dear.
**Mother Shipton** What do you mean, "oh dear"? Thanks to them—(*referring to the audience*)—he's dropped off. Now we've got time to think.
**The Great Boon** It's not that. They've all come to experience the excitement and thrill of the Circus and the Circus hasn't arrived and in the present situation we could hardly perform anyway.
**Mother Shipton** I'm sure they'll understand. (*She has an idea*) Listen, maybe they could help us again. Children, gather round. Let's all (*taking in Children and audience*)—think of a way to get rid of that great fat Giant.

*At this stage, the audience can be asked for their ideas. If it is felt this will hold up the action, or if the cast feel ill-equipped to improvize, the Children can make suggestions. The following are ideas*

**Child** The Great Boon could magic him away.
**The Great Boon** But if I do that—and there's no guarantee he won't wake up before I'm due for another spell—your home would disappear too.
**Child 2** We could tie him up with the shoelace.
**Mother Shipton** It wouldn't be big enough.
**Child 3** He might go back to his castle when he wakes up.
**Mother Shipton** But he's bound to take the shoe with him.
**Child 4** We could move the shoe to another part of the forest.

**Jill** It's too heavy.

**Child 5** Could we poison him?

**Mother Shipton** We haven't any poison. Anyway, he's bound to wake up if we went climbing up him to reach his mouth.

*These are suggestions—the audience may have wilder and more bloodthirsty ones. All ideas must be shown to be not foolproof*

**Mother Shipton** (*eventually*) Now come on, think, think, think.

**The Great Boon** Could we not frighten him off somehow? He must be frightened of *something*.

*Cocky suddenly clucks with excitement*

**Mother Shipton** Shh, Cocky, we're thinking.

*Cocky clucks more*

**Jill** He's got an idea.

*Cocky goes to the tree and indicates an apple*

The magic tree?

*Cocky shakes his head*

The apple?

*Cocky nods*

Something to do with the apple?

**Mother Shipton** How can we frighten the Giant off with an apple?

**Jack** Throw it at him?

**Jill** No, I've got it. Jack, remember yesterday— at the well—you took a bite of an apple?

**Jack** Ugh, yes—it was all rotten. It had a creepy crawly inside.

**Jill** Exactly—and I showed the creepy crawly to the Giant and—

**Jack** (*understanding*)—and his knees went all wobbly and he ran off going "Aaaaaaaah!" He was terrified.

**Jill** All we have to do to get rid of him is show him a creepy crawly.

**Jack** Let's look for one. (*Calling to the Children*) Creepy crawly hunt everyone—maggots, spiders, caterpillars.

*The Children start to move off*

**Mother Shipton** (*rather loudly*) Hang on! Hang on!

*All stop. Stirring noises are heard from the Giant*

(*In a loud whisper*) When your creepy crawly scared off the Giant, he wasn't a giant, was he?

**Jack** Eh?

**Mother Shipton** He was a whittled down, special reduction economy size giant, wasn't he?

**Jill** Yes.

**Mother Shipton** And he's not now. Stuff a creepy crawly in front of his nose and he'll hardly see it.

*Pause. Jill is deflated for a while*

**The Great Boon** We need a *giant* creepy crawly—a giant caterpillar ...
**Jill** (*after a pause*) I know! Us! Get a sheet, everyone.

*Cocky clucks*

Yes, you can join in, Cocky ...
**Mother Shipton** What are you up to?
**Jill** We're going to make a giant Cockypillar!

*All the Children get a sheet*

SONG 8: **Creepy Crawly Cockypillar**

**Children**     Let's terrify the Giant
                 Make him squirm, make him sweat
                 Let's teach him a lesson
                 That he won't forget

*The Children place sheets over themselves, and using Cocky as leader, become a Loch Ness Monster Conga-like segmented creature. The sheets should not yet cover their heads, which could muffle singing. The Children dance, Cocky leading them wherever is suitable—even the auditorium. Jack and Jill could supervise the Cockypillar rather than be part of it*

                 Creepy crawly
                 Gooey and grimy
                 Slithery slidy
                 Slippery slimy
                 Wriggly wiggly
                 Icky icky ick
                 Creepy crawly
                 Cockypillar
                 Will do the trick.

*Dance*

                 Let's terrify the Giant
                 Make his blood freeze with fright
                 His heart skip a beat and
                 All his hair turn white.

                 Creepy crawly
                 Gooey and grimy
                 Slithery slidy
                 Slippery slimy
                 Wriggly wiggly
                 Icky icky ick
                 Creepy crawly

Cockypillar
Will make him sick.
He'll shiver and shake
And quiver and quake
'Mercy' he'll beg
As we slither up his leg.

Creepy crawly
Gooey and grimy
Slithery slidy
Slippery slimy
Wriggly wiggly
Icky icky ick
Creepy crawly
Cockypillar
Will make him sick.

Creepy crawly
Cockypillar
Will do the trick.

*The music continues as the Cockypillar, encouraged by Mother Shipton and The Great Boon, moves towards the Giant's feet and exits L, as though crawling up his leg*

*Tension chord as the others wait for a reaction, watching anxiously. Sudden snorts come from the Giant, leading to an enormous roar*

**Giant** Aaaaaaah! A crawly creepy, creepy crawly! Aaaaaaaah!

*The two feet disappear. The Giant is heard getting up. Mother Shipton and Jack and Jill are jubilant. (Mother Shipton's ensuing lines echo the action. They may be found to be unnecessary)*

**Mother Shipton** They've done it!

*They follow the Giant's progress, as it were, accompanied by booming footsteps over the speakers. First the steps get softer as he goes away from them. They are relieved*

He's going.

*The steps get louder, as though he is coming back*

**The Great Boon** He's coming back!

*They react accordingly, then follow the footsteps as they cross, as it were, the auditorium, behind the audience, then to the magic tree. With frightening grunting noises the Giant is heard climbing the tree off stage, while the part of the tree that can be seen shakes as it takes the weight*

**Mother Shipton** He's climbing the magic tree!

*It is clear from Mother Shipton's face that the plan has gone awry*

*The Cockypillar enters R—having gone round behind the stage—as though it has just chased the Giant*

*The Lights change excitingly to suggest the swaying tree, which creaks menacingly. The Children remove their sheets and look up. The music continues*

Look out, children, it's coming down!

*The following sequence becomes almost nightmarish—controlled hysteria. Bedlam, as the Children scream and run around terrified. Mother Shipton, The Great Boon, Jack and Jill try in vain to control them. Cocky clucks and flaps his wings. Mother Shipton, realizing that the tree and Giant could come down on top of the shoe, vainly tries to push the shoe away. Others join her, but to no avail. Finally Mother Shipton forces all the Children and Cocky to "safety"— as far over down L as possible. All huddle helpless, just as an enormous Giant's club tumbles down from the flies, as though the Giant has dropped it. If this is impracticable, a giant handkerchief may be substituted. From now on the dialogue is audible, but the creaking of the tree and the Giant's grunts continue, sustaining the tension*

(*Shouting*) Do something, Mr Great Boon.
**The Great Boon** (*shouting*) I can't, madam. No spell for hours yet.
**Jack** *Try*!
**Jill** *Please*!
**The Great Boon** Very well. Maybe if everybody—(*taking in the Children and audience*)—joined in and really concentrated hard, a spell might work. Will you join in?
**Children** Yes } *Speaking*
**Audience**       *together*
**The Great Boon** After me, then. (*He takes up his pose and magic wand*) Jiggery pokery.
**All** Jiggery pokery.
**The Great Boon** Oink, ink, ink.
**All** Oink, ink, ink.
**The Great Boon** Pokery jiggery.
**All** Pokery jiggery.
**The Great Boon** (*Waving the wand furiously towards the Giant*) Shrink, shrink, shrink.
**All** Shrink, shrink, shrink.

*Flash. Blackout. Music. The tree creaks and Giant's grunts stop. When the Lights come up, the shoe and the giant club have disappeared. The tree is no longer shaking. Mother Shipton is hiding her eyes, holding on to Cocky and trembling*

**Jill** He's done it!
**Jack** Well done. Mr Great Boon!

*Cheers*

**The Great Boon** It couldn't have been accomplished without your—(*taking in the audience*)—invaluable assistance. I was very lucky. Thank you.

*Mother Shipton emerges. The Children wander across the stage, relieved*

**Mother Shipton** Is it safe?
**Jill** Yes, Mother. The Giant's gone.
**Mother Shipton** And our home?
**The Great Boon** A necessary inconvenience in the circumstances, madam.
**Mother Shipton** Yes, yes. (*Sad but resigned*) I understand, Mr Great Boon.
**The Great Boon** I'm sorry. (*He produces a bunch of flowers*) For you.
**Mother Shipton** Thank you. (*Without conviction*) Most kind. I must put them
   in water.

*Cocky clucks, indicating the place where the giant shoe was. All gather round
to look. A child picks up a very small shoe and hands it to Mother Shipton*

**Jack** It's the shoe! It's tiny, look!
**The Great Boon** Abracadabbages, you mean it hasn't disappeared altogether?
**Jill** No. But it's much smaller than last time.
**Mother Shipton** Then what about the Giant?
**The Great Boon** Elementary logic, madam. The Giant, too, must have been
   reduced in size. Like the shoe.
**Mother Shipton** (*thinking it through*) But if the shoe's shrunk smaller than
   it was last time ...
**Child** Look!

*The Child holds up a mini-club, or handkerchief. All think what this means.
Music*

   *The Mini-Giant enters—a miniature version played by a tiny child complete
   with beard. He either climbs down part of the magic tree, or has evidently
   climbed down off stage. He is shaking his fists furiously, and trying to look
   frightening*

*All start laughing at the Mini-Giant, who looks so helpless and harmless*

**The Great Boon** We've well and truly cut the Giant down to size!
**Jack** He's a Mini-Giant!
**Mother Shipton** Serves him right. (*Bending down to him*) You've been a very,
   very naughty Giant—kicking all our cottages down.
**Jill** Trampling on the trees.
**Mother Shipton** Kidnapping all these children's mums and dads.

*Cocky clucks*

   And Cocky.

*The Mini-Giant turns to see Cocky looming over him. He falls to his knees beg-
ging for mercy*

   What have you got to say for yourself?

*The Mini-Giant opens and shuts his mouth*

**The Great Boon** I think he's shrunk so much he's lost his voice. (*He bends
   down and listens to the Mini-Giant*) He's saying "mercy, mercy"
**Jack** He's never shown much "mercy, mercy".

**The Great Boon** I have a splendid idea. He can come and work for me in the Circus. I need a small assistant for my new miraculous illusion. Agreed?

*The Mini-Giant nods*

And if you're good I'll magic your voice back for you. (*He leads him to his caravan*) Right, in there, and get ready.

*The Mini-Giant goes inside the caravan*

**Jack** Ready? What for?

**The Great Boon** To perform. (*Looking out front*) They won't wait much longer, they'll go home. We mustn't let them down. It's time for the Circus.

**Jill** But there isn't a Circus.

**The Great Boon** There is.

**Jack** Where? I can't see it.

**The Great Boon** You. All of you.

*The Children react excited*

**Mother Shipton** What's happening?

**The Great Boon** Mother Shipton. To my caravan if you please. You must be Ringmaster. I beg your pardon, Ringmistress.

*Cocky clucks*

And Cocky. Find a costume too. Performing pet cockerel.

*Cocky excitedly goes to the caravan, trying to push Mother Shipton in front of him*

**Mother Shipton** But—Cocky!

**The Great Boon** Everyone else too.

*The Children all go to the caravan. If possible it is "parked" in such a way that they can exit through it. It might then look as though the caravan is accommodating all of them. Otherwise Jack and Jill could supervise the Children up stage, giving them whatever circus costume—a ruff, a hat—they need*

*The Great Boon turns to the audience. Fanfare*

Ladies and gentlemen, young ladies, young gentlemen. Welcome to the one and only—

*Fanfare*

*Mother Shipton emerges from the caravan. Jack and Jill slap a top hat on her and hand her a whip. She still does not quite understand*

—Mother Shipton's Children's Circus!

*Mother Shipton is pushed forward into the "ring"*

*The Great Boon returns to the caravan*

*If required, the set can, during the following song, become more and more circus-like—all provided, as it were, by The Great Boon's caravan. Some productions might run to a sign—"Mother Shipton's Children's Circus" in flashing lights overhead. But the improvisatory nature of the Circus must never be lost*

*As Mother Shipton, confused, stumbles into the "ring" the lights narrow down on to her—possibly into a follow-spot*

**Mother Shipton** But I . . . oh, all right—here goes!

SONG 9: **The Show's the Thing** (*Part 1*)

(*Singing*)                 The Ringmaster, the Juggler
                            The Strongman, the Trapeze
                            The Lions, Tigers, Elephants
                            And clever Chimpanzees,
                            The Bare Back Riders, Acrobats,
                            The White-faced Clown
                            No doubt about it
                            The Circus is in town.

*The Lights come up and the "ring" becomes a hive of activity. The Great Boon, stage-managing like mad, sends on all the performers—the Children with Jack and Jill—to join Mother Shipton. They wear ruffs, hats etc. to suggest circus costumes, or they play animals, with a mask. During the song, everybody mimes various circus tricks e.g. juggling, tightrope-walking. Clearly if any of the cast have special skills they should use them and perform for real—walking on stilts, unicycling, somersaults: but in this part of the song it is the general busy scene that is important rather than the highlighting of an individual act*

**All**                     The show's the thing
                            To make you smile
                            Forget your worries
                            For a little while
                            There's something in the magic of the circus ring
                            So have a fling
                            Stop worrying.

                            The music starts
                            The lights begin to fade
                            The audience awaits the grand parade
                            Suddenly you're in a land of make believe
                            And once you're there
                            You'll never want to leave.

                            The tension on the high trapeze
                            When he almost falls
                            It makes you freeze
                            You love to see the antics of the funny clown
                            And roar with laughter when they knock him down.

                            The animals all do amazing tricks
                            The horses dance and even do high kicks
                            It's a type of entertainment that can never flop
                            The scintillating magic of the Big Top.

*Everyone accompanies Mother Shipton, singing "Ah"*

**Mother Shipton**    The glitter, the glamour, the fun of disguise
                      The stunning, the thrilling, the gasp of surprise
                      The laughter, the slapstick, the daring, the bold,
**All**               The Circus has appeal for young and old.

*The music continues as the Circus acts begin. These acts will clearly vary from production to production, and be tailored to the talents and skills of the cast. Mother Shipton remains as the Ringmistress and, if necessary, introduces each act—using the Children's real names. The following ideas are no more than a very vague guideline but the whole Circus should probably not last longer than ten minutes or so*

1. Cocky's dance—short, strutting, amusing.
2. An acrobatic "troupe".
3. A choreographed "animal" act—with Mother Shipton as the trainer.
4. An Instrumental (Music) act.
5. A Trampoline act.
6. Strongman—Half a dozen Children stagger on with a set of dumbbells—apparently very heavy. They position them. Enter Jack as muscle-rippling strongman. He exerts himself to pick up the dumbbells, accompanied by dramatic drum rolls. He holds them above his head. Mother Shipton leads the applause. But then he falls backwards with the "weight" and the dumbbells fall across his neck. Mother Shipton is concerned, but immediately a very small child rushes on and with one hand removes the feather light dumbbells and runs off smiling. Jack covers his embarrassment and exits.

7. Clowns—    Carrying a bucket of "Water" balanced on a pole—dangerously near the audience. When bucket tips up, it is attached to the pole and streamers fall out.

*or*           Well-rehearsed slapstick act—for three children—A, B and C.

              Music as A. and B. enter as Clowns. They set a floor cloth, then exit again. C. enters as a Clown, hands behind his back—holding, concealed, two custard pies. A. and B. return, each carrying two custard pies. They nudge each other—indicating "Lets get C." They stand next to C., A. to his R and B. to his L. From now on each movement is very slow and deliberate.
              1. B. nudges C., who turns towards him.
              2. B. deliberately bangs the custard pie in his right hand against C.'s face.
              3. Both face front again. B. smiles.
              4. A. nudges C. who turns towards him.
              5. A. deliberately bangs the custard pie in his left hand against C.'s face.
              6. Both face front again. A. smiles.

7. B. and A. knowingly weigh up their remaining custard pies.
8. C. looks from L to R, knowing more pies are coming.
9. B. and A. raise their left and right hands respectively, preparing to fire.
10. At the exact moment that they fire C. ducks.
11. The two pies of B. and A. meet as their hands meet in the air over C.'s head.
12. All three straighten again. The used pies are dropped.
13. B. and A. in unison, look at each hand in turn—no pies. They now look vulnerable.
14. C. produces his two pies from behind his back. He smiles.
15. At the same moment as each other, B. and A. notice C.'s two pies. They react, anticipating the worst.
16. C., using just his eyes and a nod, asks the audience whether he should use his pies. A. and B. shake their heads.
17. Suddenly, preferably when the audience least expect it, C. lands both pies—one on A's face, and one on B.'s face. Chord of music as they exit.

8. 'Animals'— Seals (heading a ball) dogs through paper hoops.
9. Walking on hands: pogo-stick jumping: cartwheels: skate-boarding: unicycling.
10. Roller-skating ballet.
11. Tap-dancing.
12. The Great Boon's Magic Act. (See notes for a suggested "Ghost-to-Witch illusion on p. viii)

This will probably only be used when the Children in the production are not very talented—which will doubtless be a rare event. The Circus is best used to develop and present the Children's abilities, rather than The Great Boon's.

*It must be emphasized that these are very basic ideas, and must be evolved by the Director and the Company in rehearsal, using what talents are available, or using mime and dance skills to suggest circus skills*

*As the acts come to an end, Mother Shipton steps forward*

**Mother Shipton** And now, for the first time in any circus ring, the amazing, incredible magic of—The Great Boon and the Mini-giant!

*The Great Boon and Mini-Giant enter. The Great Boon magically makes the Mini-Giant "vanish". (See note on p. viii) As the "vanish" takes place the Mini-Giant reappears somewhere impossible—perhaps at the back of the auditorium, and runs on to take applause*

*Music, as the Children rush forward for their Finale*

SONG 9: (*cont.*)

**All** (*singing*)        The show's the thing
                     To make you smile

Forget your worries
For a little while
There's something in the magic of a circus ring,
So ...

*The song is interrupted, as suddenly a very loud bell sounds—all stop. The Great Boon takes out his alarm clock and turns off the bell.*

**The Great Boon** Spell-time! Now, children, how can I thank you for providing such a splendid Circus.

*A Child comes forward*

**Child** Please, Mr Great Boon, we'd like to see our mums and dads again.
**The Great Boon** Of course you would! And now the Giant works for me, he has no need for his slaves any more. Now—let's see.

*Drum roll, as The Great Boon takes his pose and waves his wand*

Jiggery Pokery
Clacketty Clack
Pokery Jiggery
Parents come back!

*Dramatic pause. Nothing happens. All look at each other, concerned. The Great Boon decides to try again*

Come on, everyone. (*Taking in the audience too*). Help me. (*He encourages them to repeat the spell a line at a time*)

**All**       Jiggery Pokery
Clacketty Clack
Pokery Jiggery
Parents come back!

*Pause. Nothing*

**The Great Boon** (*very sincerely*) Apologies, children, I think I must have used up all my spells.
**Mother Shipton** Never mind, Mr Great Boon. You did your best.

*Music, as the Children sadly accept the spell is not going to work*

SONG 10: **Finale**

| | |
|---|---|
| **All** (*singing*) | There was an old woman |
| **Mother Shipton** | That's me |
| **All** | Who lived in a shoe |
| | She had so many children |
| **Children** | That's us |
| **All** | She didn't know what to |
| | Cockadoodle ... |

*All suddenly stop as from offstage or over the speakers are heard footsteps running and adult cries of "Children, Children", "There they are". All look off, or out front, to see what is happening. Then the Children's faces show that they can see their parents*

**Jack** You've done it, Mr Great Boon, you've done it!

*As the adult voices call each child's name, he or she runs happily off, or through the auditorium, to meet his or her parents. Some stop to hug Mother Shipton or wave to Jack, Jill, Cocky and The Great Boon*

*The remaining characters step forward*

| | |
|---|---|
| **Mother Shipton** | And Jack |
| | And Jill |
| **All** | Cockadoodle Doo. |

*The music continues under the dialogue. The characters remaining naturally have mixed emotions*

**Mother Shipton** (*calling after the Children*) 'Bye, children. 'Bye. I'll miss you.
**The Great Boon** As I said yesterday, madam, all good stories have a happy ending.

*Mother Shipton nods sadly*

**Mother Shipton** (*in tears*) Very happy.
**Jill** Come on, Mother, at least you'll be able to cope now.
**Jack** Yes, there won't be nearly so much washing, polishing, mending, scrubbing, sweeping, cooking, cleaning, fetching, carrying, sewing, lifting, stretching and bending to do.

*Mother Shipton smiles*

**Mother Shipton** No, dear. And I've still got you two.

*Cocky clucks*

And you, Cocky. Come on, let's go home. (*She turns, as if to enter the shoe: suddenly she realizes it is not there*) Oo-er. I forgot. We're still homeless. Come to that, so are all the children and their mums and dads.

*The Mini-Giant comes forward and tugs The Great Boon's sleeve. He whispers in his ear*

**The Great Boon** What? Oh, really? Splendid. (*To Mother Shipton*) Madam, my new assistant has invited all of you and all the children and their parents to live in his castle. After all, from now on he'll be touring the world with yours truly. And it's too big for him now anyway.
**Mother Shipton** Thank you. We accept. No hard feelings. Well, not too many, anyway. (*She shakes hands with the Mini-Giant*)
**Jill** Maybe we should let him have his shoe back?

*Jack produces the shoe*

**Mother Shipton** Why not?

*The Mini-Giant receives his shoe and slips it on*

**The Great Boon** We must be off. Maybe one day we'll find the real Circus, though I'll never forget Mother Shipton's Children's Circus.

**Mother Shipton** Thank you for everything, Mr Great Boon.

**The Great Boon** My pleasure, madam. (*He produces a bunch of flowers for her*) For you.

**Mother Shipton** Thank you. I must put them in water.

**All** (*singing*)

    Cockadoodle Doo

**Mother Shipton** ⎫
**and Family** ⎭   It's time to be off, now we've lost the shoe   ⎰ *Singing*
                                                                       ⎱ *together*

**All** (*taking in the audience*)
    It's time to say goodbye
    Goodbye to all of you
    Cockadoodle Doo.

*The two groups, Mother Shipton and family, and The Great Boon and Mini-Giant, exit on opposite sides, as—*

                 *the* CURTAIN *falls*

CURTAIN CALL

*The whole cast rush on singing*

SONG 10A: **Curtain call—The Show's the Thing** (*Part 2*)

**All**    The show's the thing
To make you smile
Forget your worries
For a little while
There's something in the magic of the circus ring
So have a fling
Stop worrying.

The music starts
The lights begin to fade
The audience awaits the grand parade
Suddenly you're in a land of make believe
And once you're there
You'll never want to leave.

The tension on the high trapeze
When he almost falls
It makes you freeze
You love to see the antics of the funny clown
And roar with laughter when they knock him down.

The animals all do amazing tricks
The horses dance and even do high kicks
It's a type of entertainment that can never flop
The scintillating magic of the Big Top.

The glitter, the glamour, the fun of disguise
The stunning, the thrilling, the gasp of surprise
The laughter, the slapstick, the daring, the bold,
The circus has appeal for young and old.

Our time is up
We've got to go
We hope that you've
Enjoyed the show
It's time to take our costumes off
And make-up too
Turn out the lights
And say good night to you.

And as we take our final bow
We'll say one thing right here and now
The show's the thing
To make you sing

The show's the thing
To beat ev'rything
With an audience the actors can make it swing
The show's the thing.

CURTAIN

# FURNITURE AND PROPERTY LIST

## ACT I

*On stage:* Giant shoe used as house, with windows, door, chimney, window-boxes, long shoelaces
Normal-sized shoe (concealed)
Pail

*Off stage:* Sheets (**Children**)
Broom (**Mother Shipton**)
Pile of enamel plates or bowls (**Jack**)
Packet of cornflakes (**Jill**)
Caravan with bell or horn (**The Great Boon**)
Water-well, apple tree, loose apples (**Stage Management**)
Human-size club (**Giant**)
Magical apple tree (**Stage Management**)
Giant bare foot (**Stage Management**)

*Personal:* **Mother Shipton:** whistle
**The Great Boon:** silk handkerchief with mini-feathers wrapped inside. trick bunch of flowers, wand, loud alarm clock, other trick items
**Giant:** rope

## ACT II

*Set:* Pieces of chalk by shoe (optional)
Pieces of clothing with words of song, pegs (optional)
Very small shoe (concealed)
Broom stick in caravan (for optional magic illusion)

*Off stage:* Shoe-clad Giant's foot (**Stage Management**)
Giant's bare foot (**Stage Management**)
Silk handkerchiefs with words of song, hat (**The Great Boon**—optional)
Sheets (**Children**)
Giant's club, or handkerchief (**Stage Management**)
Small club or handkerchief (**Stage Management**—to set in Black-out)
Top hat, whip (**Jack, Jill**)
Various items as desired for Circus acts (**Children**)

*Personal:* **Great Boon:** 2 trick bunches of flowers

# LIGHTING PLOT

Note: The following plot covers cues included in the text. Spots and other effects during songs, etc., may be added at the Director's discretion

Property fittings required: nil
Exteriors. A Forest Glade. A Hilltop

ACT I      Dawn
*To open:*   General effect of breaking dawn

| | | |
|---|---|---|
| *Cue* 1: | As CURTAIN rises<br>*Slow fade up to full daylight* | (Page 1) |
| *Cue* 2: | **Great Boon** starts to exit<br>*Change to dramatic shadowy lighting* | (Page 12) |
| *Cue* 3: | **Great Boon:** "... shrink, shrink, SHRINK"<br>*Flash; black-out, then return to opening lighting* | (Page 13) |
| *Cue* 4: | At general exit after "Cockadoodle Doo" song<br>*Cross-fade to water-well lighting* | (Page 14) |
| *Cue* 5: | **Jack** and **Jill** exit<br>*Cross-fade to previous lighting* | (Page 18) |
| *Cue* 6: | **Great Boon:** "... for tummy, tum tum"<br>*Flash, black-out, then bring up lighting on apple tree* | (Page 20) |
| *Cue* 7: | During last verse of "Grow" song<br>*Slow general fade to dusk, eventually concentrating on* **Mother Shipton** *and* **Children** | (Page 22) |
| *Cue* 8: | During "Till today becomes tomorrow" song<br>*Fade to night (optional—bring up moon and stars)* | (Page 23) |
| *Cue* 9: | After **Children** settle down to sleep<br>*Slow fade up to morning light* | (Page 23) |
| *Cue* 10: | **Jill:** "Stop, stop!"<br>*Flash, black-out, then return to continuing fade up to daylight* | (Page 26) |

## ACT II

*To open:*   Light concentrated on shoe area

| | | |
|---|---|---|
| *Cue* 11: | At end of opening verse<br>*Fade up to morning light* | (Page 29) |
| *Cue* 12: | **Cockypillar** enters<br>*Cross-fade to menacing shadowy effect on magic tree* | (Page 35) |

Cue 13:    **All:** "Shrink, shrink, shrink"                          (Page 36)
           *Flash, black-out, then up to morning light*

Cue 14:    **Mother Shipton** is pushed into circus ring        (Page 39)
           *Fade to spot on* **Mother Shipton**

Cue 15:    **Mother Shipton:** "The Circus is in town"           (Page 39)
           *Fade up to full overall lighting*

# EFFECTS PLOT

## ACT I

*Cue* 1: At end of "Cockadoodledoo" song      (Page 4)
*Smoke rises from chimney*

*Cue* 2: **Great Boon** starts to exit      (Page 12)
*Giant footsteps, becoming gradually louder*

*Cue* 3: As **Mother Shipton** tries to push shoe off      (Page 13)
*Loud alarm clock rings*

*Cue* 4: **Mother Shipton:** "... away for a start"      (Page 19)
*Loud alarm clock rings*

*Cue* 5: **Children** chase off L, after **Giant**      (Page 24)
*Loud alarm clock rings*

## ACT II

*Cue* 6: **Jack:** "Foot two. Without shoe"      (Page 29)
*Giant footsteps moving around*

*Cue* 7: **Mother Shipton:** "Thank goodness"      (Page 29)
*Loud crash*

*Cue* 8: After **Giant** gets up      (Page 35)
*Giant footsteps moving around*

*Cue* 9: **All:** "... in the magic of a circus ring: So..."      (Page 42)
*Loud alarm clock rings*